You Can Draw Horses

This book is about horses and how to draw them. You can draw them from life at the stables, from reference at home, or even straight from your imagination. It doesn't matter as long as you are drawing and enjoying it.

Making a start

The first thing to do is to try and see a real horse. Maybe you have a riding stables near you that you could visit or maybe there is an urban farm or a field with horses in. It will make a tremendous difference just looking at the real thing.

Horse box

Start a collection of horse photographs. Cut them out of magazines and newspapers and store them in a box or book. This will be the beginning of your reference library.

Step by Step Horses

To draw horses well, it is essential to draw one from life. Then you can observe closely how a horse moves and behaves. It might help to get to know your subject a little first and that is really the idea behind these drawings.

👁 Observe

Look at these step-by-step drawings and try copying them, gradually building up a complete drawing of a horse. I started with two ovals, a large one for the body and a small one for the head. Then flesh out the neck and legs from your initial lines and add the details last.

⭐ Tip

If you struggle with a particular part of the body, like the ears or head, make separate studies of these until you feel confident.

lined paper

packaging

brown paper

tracing paper

ink stain

old book
lightly painted over
with white

📖 On the hoof

If you want to become good at drawing horses,
or anything else, then it is vital to keep a sketchbook.
You can make this by clipping some paper together or you can buy
one. Take your sketchbook with you wherever you go and draw what
you see. Start with a collection of drawings of horses' hooves.
Copy from paintings, photographs and from life. Look at your
reference box (page 1). You'll soon know how to draw them.

☆ Tip

An excellent idea is to prepare each sketchbook double page with
a surface or background. You'll find these great fun to draw on
and drawing tools will respond in different ways to these surfaces,
so experiment to find successful combinations. There are some
suggestions on this page, and more tips throughout the book.

magazines
lightly painted
over with white

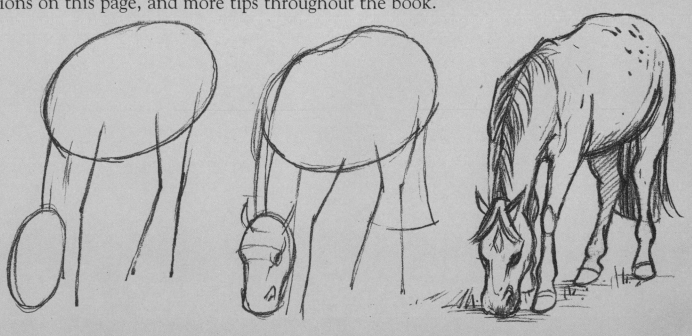

More Step by Step Horses

Here are two more pages of step-by-step horses to help you to practise.

As your confidence grows, try leaving out some of the simple earlier stages.

Observe
Notice how the right back and front hooves and the left front and back hooves line up in all of the drawings.

The mane and tail are fun to draw but try to get the proportions of your horse right first.

Aim to be adventurous when you work on your drawings. Try as many different tools as you can so you get to know how each works and what effect you can achieve with it.

★ Tip

Pencils range from 6H, the hardest, to 6B, the softest, with HB exactly in the middle. A soft pencil lets you blur the line and is ideal for thick, expressive strokes but try not to make your drawing woolly. Never use anything harder than an HB to draw like this with.

You can add tones (shading) either by using an ordinary pencil, or a water-soluble pencil like an Aquarelle, by running a wet brush over the line as in the drawing (left) of the heavy horse.

Horses at Home

brush pen

These drawings were made from a toy model horse. This is excellent practice and will give you a real idea of the shape, proportions and anatomy of a horse before you attempt to draw a real one from life. You can buy them from most toy shops.

dip pen

fibre-tip pen

Drawing tool

This drawing was made with a fibre-tip pen. The shading is made by cross-hatching. A limitation of this pen is that the line is always the same thickness. Compare the marks of the fibre-tip pen and those of the dip pen.

fountain pen

Observe

The detail on these toy models is often superb, so look closely while you draw.

Model pupil

Try building up a collection of drawings from models; maybe make a series of small books, one for each model. This kind of drawing is called `observational drawing'. It is excellent practice to look at something three-dimensional and try to keep this solidity in your two-dimensional drawing.

Drawing tool
These drawings were made using a fountain pen (see page 12).

Key point
I have made a drawing from every angle of this model, turning it round a little more each time and starting again.

Heads

If you make detailed studies of all parts of the horse's body, this will help you to understand exactly what it looks like. Here are two pages of heads to copy. A horse is symmetrical in shape so this is a big help.

gift wrap painted over with white

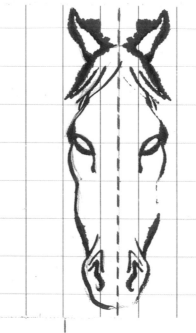

☆ Tip

Try drawing half a horse's head on a piece of paper with paint. If you are quick and fold the paper over before the paint is dry, the other half of your horse's head will print. This shows it is symmetrical.

brown paper

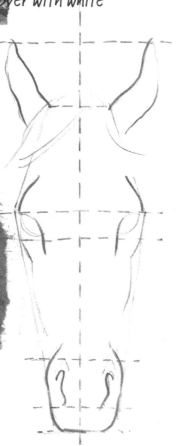

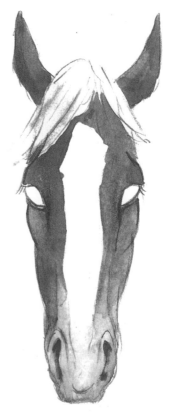

👁 Observe

Look at the horse's head front on (see opposite). Draw the ears, eyes and nostrils. It sometimes helps to measure the distance between these features.

tea or coffee stain

☝ Key point

Measure like this: hold your pencil so that it lines up with the top of the horse's head. Now gradually slide your thumb down the pencil until it lines up with the horse's mouth. This gives you the length of the horse's head. Turn your pencil so that it's horizontal for the distance between the eyes, ears, etc. You can draw the entire horse, or anything else for that matter, by measuring like this.

ink stain

Drawing from Photographs

It is always better to draw from the living animal but if this isn't possible, a good quality photograph is second best.

☞ Key point
Firstly, make sure it is a good quality photograph that shows plenty of detail.

☆ Tip
Try making several drawings from one photograph using different drawing tools. Compare your drawings and try to analyse which works best and why.

Drawing tool
For the drawing of this pony, I used a mixture of different media: ink, pencil, watercolour, and gouache (paint). It helps to make this drawing really exciting and alive.

11

Photo fit

If you have a camera it is a good idea to take a photograph of the horse you are drawing from life. You can refer to this later at home. Write on the back where you drew the horse and any other information you can find out, like what breed it is, its name and how old it is.

Tip
To help to keep your drawing lively, try looking at the photograph for a few minutes. Then turn it over and draw from memory.

Key point
Remember that the horse is a living three-dimensional animal, not a two-dimensional cut-out so try to make your drawing solid.

At the Stables

A great way to study horses close up is to visit a riding stables. Check that the stable owners don't mind you drawing there and go well prepared. Take your sketchbook and maybe even some larger paper. Take a varied selection of drawing tools and wear something warm. When you sit drawing for a long time outside you'll be surprised how cold you can get even on a sunny day.

Drawing tool

Here I've used a fountain pen to draw with. It is excellent for taking on location. It doesn't dry up, you can smudge the ink with water and it easily fits in your pocket.

Key point

Try to begin a drawing within five minutes of arriving.
If you spend too much time wandering around thinking
about what to draw, you could end up doing nothing. If
you start quickly you are much more likely to have a
successful day. The more you draw, the easier it will be.

Tip

It is best to choose
just one horse and
draw it many times. Then
you'll get to know it and your
drawings will improve.
    Never sit closely behind a horse.
Sit where it can see you and be careful not to
startle it with sudden movements or noises such as
turning over large sheets of paper. Horses' temperaments
vary just like ours and the stable owner will probably tell
you which horse will not like being drawn.

Drawing from Life

When you draw from life, it is unlikely that you will end up with one complete drawing of a horse. More usual will be pages of drawings of heads, bodies, feet all half started and jumbled together. As you can see on these two pages, the drawings I made of horses in a field are just like that. But all the information I need to draw a completed horse is here.

⭐ Tip

Make written notes as well as drawings. Try to record colour. Use arrows to point to details that are repeated rather than draw them over and over again.

Horses for courses

You will only find out which drawing tool is best for the job by experimenting. Try them out in your sketchbook. Here are some tips on drawing tools and what they might do.

Charcoal. Use the side for thick, broad areas of shading and the tip for drawing. Charcoal will give a huge range of tones from deepest black to pale, pale grey but your drawing will need fixing to stop it smudging. You can buy fixative or use hairspray.

Fibre-tip pen. Clean and easy to use, best for drawing on location where too many materials would be impractical (see page 6).

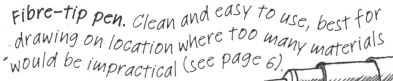

Dip pen. Fabulous for lively drawings but you will need practice. You will also need to carry a bottle of Indian ink which you should dilute with distilled water.

Ball point. Great for quick drawings in difficult, busy locations.

Wax crayon. Best for large drawings as it is difficult to draw small details with wax crayons.

Marker pen. I like to use these when they are running out as they make a more varied mark. Again better for quite big drawings.

Cartoon Horses

Here are a few tips on how to draw cartoon horses. You can adapt some of your drawings or just draw straight from your head. To draw a cartoon horse you exaggerate and play with the characteristics of a real horse.

👁 Observe

Start with an oval and a circle for the body and head. Follow these step-by-step stages and gradually flesh out your drawing.

Mind my eye.

I'd rather be pink.

Personalised ponies

Make a greetings card using some of your cartoon drawings. If you can think of a joke you can include this or maybe make something like a good-luck card in a horse-shoe shape. Here are some suggestions for headings to get you thinking: Pony Post! Riding High! First past the Post!

Show off!

Key point

In the cartoon world anything goes, so your horse can walk on two legs or drive a car, or it can be pink with a blue mane. Let your imagination go into overdrive.

Horses in Action

To draw horses in action, try to freeze the image in your memory and then quickly draw it. It really helps to use something like a brush dipped in ink or a stick of charcoal because this is not about drawing detail but about capturing a moment on paper. This is very difficult and you'll probably find it easier to start by copying photographs.

👉 **Key point**

Don't worry if you find this difficult. It is. Don't give up. Your hand and eye co-ordination skills will soon improve with practice.

👁 **Observe**

Notice how the background behind this horse is blurred. This adds to the feeling of movement and energy.

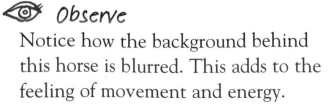

⭐ **Tip**
To try to capture the life and energy of the real thing
I've used a stick dipped in ink.

📖 *Sketchbook activity*
The key to success with drawing horses in action is to spend more
time looking at the horse and less time looking at the paper.
Practise drawing your model horses without looking at the paper.
DON'T CHEAT! You'll soon get used to not looking at your drawing
and with luck everything will be more or less in the right place.

Horses in Art

The horse was domesticated about six thousand years ago and Man has continually represented it in paintings, drawings and sculptures. There are images of horses on Greek pots, Viking tapestries, and cave paintings in Spain that date back seventeen thousand years.

Painted ponies

We can learn a lot by looking at and recording images of horses from past civilisations. Visit a museum or an art gallery with your sketchbook. Make copies of as many horses as you can. Try to record the colours and patterns. Observe how the harnesses change over time. You'll soon fill up a sketchbook.

⭐ *Tip*

When using a sketchbook, don't forget to make written notes of the things you can't draw, such as age, scale and materials. Always note where you've been, in case you want to go back.

Foals

If you are lucky enough to see a foal, don't miss the chance to draw it.

👁 Observe

In all of these drawings, start with a larger oval for the body and a smaller oval for the head. Then draw in the neck and legs. Look closely to get the proportions correct. Use lines first, then flesh them out. Add the short tail and upright mane with the final details.

⭐ Tip

Look at the proportions. It is the length of a foal's legs that give it that characteristic gangly look.

Key point

A foal's head is short in length and the nose is slightly rounded.
The tail is curly and the mane stands up like a brush. If you look carefully and observe these details, your drawing will soon improve.

Breeds

Here is a range of different breeds for you to copy. Look carefully at the differences between them.

Shire

The Shire horse is descended from the medieval war horse. It is a giant breed, strong enough to carry a knight in full armour.

Shire silhouettes

Draw an outline of a Shire horse on a piece of card and carefully cut it out. You can either use the card as a stencil and dab paint through to make an image or you can spray paint around the cut-out piece. You can even paint the cut-out piece to use as a simple print. Try making gift wrap or greetings cards with your Shire silhouettes.

Observe

The 'feather' on the feet and the massive build are both important features of the Shire horse.

Arab

A beautiful horse. The eyes and the nostrils are large and the face is slightly dipped. These details are important and will help make your drawing recognisable.

Palomino

With its white mane and golden-coloured body, the Palomino is very striking. It is all about colour so it is important to get this right.

Tack

The equipment used for riding horses is usually called 'tack'.

bridle

halter

head collar

These drawings show some of the more common pieces of tack. You will come across these when you draw horses, so if you know exactly how they fit on the horse, this will help when you draw them. Tack varies a lot, so always draw what you see.

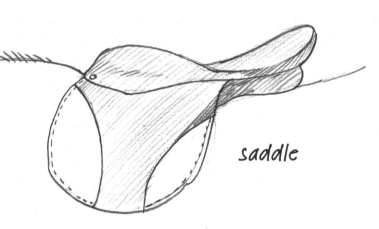

saddle

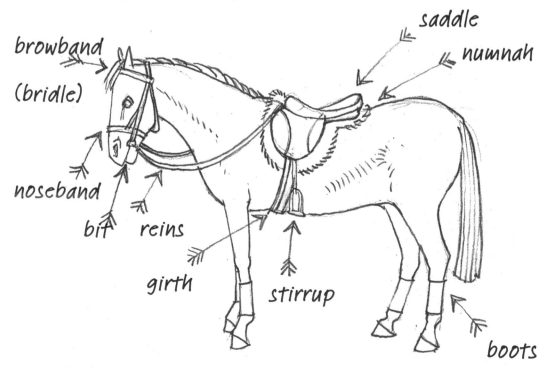

browband
(bridle)

noseband

bit   reins

girth   stirrup

saddle

numnah

boots

The tack on the horse opposite, taken from a heraldic crest, is several hundred years old but has changed little from modern tack.

The strap around the top of its front legs is called a 'martingale'. It is to stop the horse raising its head too high.

Heraldic Horses

Horses and unicorns are frequently used in heraldry and appear on crests, shields and coats of arms. They are used as logos for banks, cars, building societies and fashion houses. They are embossed on coins and stylised as figures in games like chess. Start a collection of drawings, rubbings and prints of heraldic horses. The dramatic and exaggerated nature of the horses in heraldry with their prancing legs and rearing posture make exciting subjects. They work especially well on sketchbook pages that have been prepared with patches of bright, strong colour.

Mythical Horses

Horses abound in mythology and you may feel inspired to create pictures of legendary horses like unicorns and the winged Pegasus. Let your imagination take over. The important thing in creating images like this isn't drawing the leg exactly right but whether or not the drawing is exciting and dramatic.

Pegasus

According to Greek mythology, this famous winged horse was ridden by Bellerophon in his epic battle with the Chimaera monster.

👁 Observe

It is his wings that make this drawing so exciting. Study some stuffed birds in a museum and practise drawing them to get the wings right.

✍ Key point

The wings need to be drawn big because they have a lot to carry. If the wings are too small, the drawing will look unconvincing even though it is a mythical beast.

Sleipnir

According to Norse mythology, Sleipnir was a grey colt with eight legs who galloped around the heavens (Valhalla), carrying mighty Odin on his back.

Key point

The background for both of these horses is very important in setting the scene.

⭐ Tip

Don't be afraid to have a go at drawings like these. The basic form is still just a horse. Go back to the step-by-step drawings on page 2 if necessary.

Horse and Rider

Here are some drawings of a horse and rider together. Use the step-by-step drawings to get the idea of how these two 'fit' together. It is difficult so don't expect instant success.

Key point The key to success is looking carefully and practising as much as you can.

Show off

If you can visit a horse show or a gymkhana, take your sketchbook with you. You can usually find these events listed in a local paper or ask the Pony Club (an international organisation with local branches: www.pcuk.org). Prepare your sketchbook first. Take a fountain pen if possible as it will not dry up whilst you are waiting for a horse and rider to come into view and the ink can be smudged to make a thicker line. The fountain pen can also make very varied marks and will fit easily into your pocket, so all in all it is an excellent choice for location drawing.

☆ **Tip**
Don't worry
about mistakes,
just draw what
you can.
Here are some
ideas for
correcting your
drawings if
necessary.

**white
paint**

line erased

patch

There are several ways to alter a drawing.
Here are some of the methods artists use:

• You can rub out. Draw the 'new' correct
  line before you erase the old one.

• You can use white paint to cover up
  unwanted lines.

• You can stick a patch of paper over a
  messy area.

Top Ten Tips

⭐ Study a real horse before trying to draw one.

⭐ Measure with your thumb and a pencil to help you to get the proportions right.

⭐ Use a variety of drawing tools, not just a pencil.

⭐ Draw with a brush or stick of charcoal to add life to your drawing.

⭐ Use a fountain pen when drawing on location.

⭐ When visiting a location, try to begin a drawing within five minutes.

⭐ Try to look at what you are drawing, not at the paper.

⭐ When using a sketchbook, don't forget to make written notes.

⭐ Lots of practice will improve your drawing.

⭐ Most of all, enjoy your drawing.

GOOD LUCK!